Wheels Around Inverclyde

by
Robert Grieves

© Robert Grieves 2001
First published in the United Kingdom, 2001,
by Stenlake Publishing
Telephone / Fax: 01290 551122

ISBN 1 84033 159 3

Hamilton Street, Greenock at its bustling busiest time of the week – a Saturday afternoon in the late 1920s – looking east towards Cathcart Square, where the Victoria tower is visible on the municipal buildings. This was still a period when all men wore headgear and most had the appearance of Paw Broon in his bunnet. One crosses to purchase a paper from the newsboy (standing beside Boots corner at Sugarhouse Lane), whose placard reads 'Football and Racing Results'. Heading away from the camera and following tramcar no. 5 is VS 1067, an American-built Reo bus which had been new in 1926 to the G. & G. (Glasgow & Gourock) bus company. Today it is hard to imagine such a scene, since the Oak Mall shopping centre now totally covers this site.

FOREWORD

The area of Renfrewshire known as Inverclyde covers 61 square miles and was formed as a result of local government reorganisation in 1975. Nearly two thirds of the 100,000 population live in the coastal towns of Port Glasgow, Greenock and Gourock on the south bank of the River Clyde where it widens to join the Firth. Farther south-west along the coast the ferry port of Wemyss Bay marks the boundary with Ayrshire, while Inverclyde's only inland community is Kilmacolm. All these places are represented in this little book, along with the wheels which served them and although some of the illustrations are well before our memory span, I hope that they will nonetheless prove of interest. They are a glimpse perhaps of how our parents and grandparents would have witnessed the local transport scene and as such are an important social documentary, sadly often dismissed. I'm sure many readers will remember Dunlop's buses which ran between Greenock and Largs, Jagger's lemonade lorries, or the old GMS local red buses with their cheery (and often cheeky) conductresses, while possibly some of the more elderly may just recall their schooldays when the Greenock & Port Glasgow trams were still running. But whether the scenes are familiar to you or not, I hope you will enjoy these views of yesterday's transport in Inverclyde. My thanks must go to the many local people who have assisted me with information for the book, including Jim Hunter, Anthony McNeill, Bryce Pollock and Andrew Webster. Credit also to Alan Brotchie for the photos on pages 4 and 5, to Ian Maclean for the one on page 33 (lower), to Bill Smith for those on pages 42 and 43, and to my former bus-driving colleague, Hector Soutter for those on pages 23–31 and the back cover.

Robert L. Scott, chairman of Scott's Shipbuilding & Engineering Co. Ltd., Greenock, lived in Balclutha House, Newark Street. Scott was the original owner of VS 165, a late Edwardian Wolseley/Siddeley, but later sold it to his chauffeur Andrew Webster who started his own motor garage in Houston Street during World War I. He later moved to Forsyth Street where he remained until the business closed in 1980. Webster was a Humber agent until 1936 and also dealt with Standard, Triumph and Rover cars. This scene on Loch Lomondside about 1919 shows Andrew Webster driving VS 165 on a private outing.

Looking towards Gourock from Ashton in the early 1870s from where the Royal Yacht Club is now situated. The villas on the hillside in Barrhill Road were built in the mid-nineteenth century by some of Gourock's more prosperous citizens. At this time the only public transport was provided by King's horse bus to and from Greenock, which was owned by McKimmie of Gourock from 1869. The local horse tramway did not commence until 1873, hence no rails are visible here.

The horse tramway in Greenock and Gourock was operated for over twenty years from 1873 by the Glasgow-based Vale of Clyde Tramways Company, which also ran trams between Glasgow and Govan. In early 1894 the Greenock & Port Glasgow Tramways Company took over operations and introduced a modern electric system in 1901. This view from the horse-drawn period shows Ashton, on what was probably a Sunday afternoon in the late 1890s, photographed from the yacht club at the foot of Victoria Road. The Greenock & Port Glasgow Tramways car approaching the terminus is about to pass a stationary car loading passengers for Greenock under the watchful eye of the conductor, who has stepped off to supervise. The couple on the left appear to be hurrying to catch the tram while the young girl in the foreground is oblivious to everything apart from her task of looking after a rather large-bonneted baby as she pushes the magnificent Victorian perambulator along the grassy esplanade.

Greenock & Port Glasgow Tramways car no. 31 shown new in 1904 when it entered the fleet. Within only two years this tram was rebuilt as a double decker. The photograph was taken at Ashton, and shows the company general manager Archibald Robertson (who may also be seen on page 12) with his foot on the platform step and his wife at the controls. Next to him is the local manager, A. A. Hawkins. The livery of the trams has been described as dark red with off-white or cream above. The company crest visible in this view shows the magnet and wheel insignia used on tramways owned by the British Electric Traction Company (as was the Greenock & Port Glasgow system) with the Gourock, Greenock and Port Glasgow burgh crests incorporated.

A scene from 1903 showing Greenock & Port Glasgow Tramways car no. 10 trundling along an almost deserted Albert Road, Gourock towards the terminus at Ashton. This was one of the 30 original electric trams delivered to the company in 1901 after withdrawal of the horse tramway and was also the last tram to operate when the system closed in 1929 (see page 21). The 1897 Victoria Diamond Jubilee fountain has now been relocated on the Esplanade near Ashburn Gate.

Although known for many years now as the Pierhead, this early Edwardian postcard dates from the period when the area was called Quay Head, Gourock. It shows Greenock & Port Glasgow Tramways car no. 12, built by Brush of Loughborough, travelling towards the end of the line at Ashton. Certain journeys terminated at the Pierhead and the rails of a siding parallel with the main double tracks may be seen. The general scene in Kempock Place is still quite recognisable today, although the layout of the gardens on the left has changed and the MacPherson fountain at the top of the street has been long removed. From 1902, the trams were housed in a depot at Ladyburn, Greenock, which was also used as a bus depot for Greenock Motor Services and successors until the present Inchgreen premises opened in 1955 for the Western SMT Co. Ltd.

Delivered in 1908 to the Greenock & Port Glasgow Tramways Co., this little 20-seat tram was known as a demi-car and was built by the United Electric Company of Preston. It was no. 40 in the fleet but saw relatively little service in Inverclyde, passing about 1918 to the associated Rothesay Tramways Company on the Isle of Bute, where the body was latterly used as a greenhouse at Ettrick Bay. This photo was taken in Ardgowan Street, Port Glasgow, passing Lithgow's Kingston Yard during the *Comet* centenary celebrations of 1912. One of the gentlemen pictured on the front of the car is Henry Bell, who introduced Scotland's first steamship, the *Comet*, to the Clyde in 1812. This was the first steam-powered vessel in Europe to convey fare-paying passengers. The other person is David Napier, who built the *Comet*'s boiler but was reputedly never paid for his work . . . some things never change!

Cathcart Square, Greenock.

A late 1920s scene showing Greenock & Port Glasgow Tramways top-covered double decker no. 43. An impatient Albion bus – which was also a member of the Tramway Co. fleet – is eager to overtake and waits its chance where Hamilton Street in Greenock widened into Cathcart Square. The Barr's advert on the tram is for 'aerated waters', which was the commonly-used term describing fizzy soft drinks for many years. Barr's have been aware of the value of good publicity since early in their history.

Brachelston Square, Greenock, lies at the top end of Nelson Street where it meets South Street and Inverkip Street. In Victorian and Edwardian times it was a pick-up point for passengers setting out on afternoon trips either down the coast or on the popular circular tour to Loch Thom and Inverkip (see overleaf). Barefoot boys who no doubt would have dearly loved to join the departing excursions watch the photographer, who took this view from a vantage point behind the railings fronting Orangefield Baptist Church. The photo dates from 1901, after King Edward VII gained the throne following Queen Victoria's death. This was also the year when electric street lighting – which may be seen partly installed in Nelson Street – came to Greenock. Coaches were often given individual names, a practice which continued on into the years of the motorbus, and those in this scene were called 'Lord Roberts' and 'Queen Alexandra'. The latter had tiered seating to allow passengers to see over the heads of those in front.

Apart from excursions by paddle steamer from Greenock and Gourock, another popular way to enjoy an outing around the turn of last century was to take a coach trip. These coaches were of course originally horse-drawn, like the example illustrated here which was owned by Thomas McLean of Cartsburn Street, Greenock. It is seen at the foot of Holmston Brae where Cloch Road joins the main road to Largs (the signpost points left to Gourock via the Cloch and right to Greenock). One of the more popular outings was the 'Loch Thom and Inverkip circular tour' on which several rival firms competed for business, particularly on Saturday afternoons and Sundays. McLean was one of those operators. Note that four horses were required on this tour to cope with the steep gradients involved on the climb to Loch Thom.

Robert Grieve Neill, of the prominent sugar company Neill, Dempster & Neill, at the wheel of SB 151, his French-built Delahaye 12/16 h.p. two-seater. The picture was taken in 1911 inside the grounds of Neill's home, 'Glenfield' (now a nursing home), in Bedford Street at the junction of Newark Street and Union Street, Greenock. The house visible in the background is 'The Limes' on Newark Street. Neill was an early member of the Automobile Association, whose original style of badge may be seen below the windscreen. In those days private motoring was beyond the means of most and enjoyed only by the privileged few such as businessmen like Neill.

VS 213 was one of the earliest purpose-built motorbuses in the Greenock area. In 1912 three similar Tilling Stevens 'petrol–electric' vehicles were delivered to the Greenock & Port Glasgow Tramways Co. with short-lived 'toastrack' style open bodywork by Fleming & Taylor of Airdrie. This was replaced in 1914 by a more conventional bus body, built locally by John Mitchell of Grey Place. The route operated by these buses ran from the tram terminus at Ashton to Inverkip, with the idea to extend later through to Largs and Ardrossan. Archibald Robertson, manager of the Greenock & Port Glasgow Tramways Co., is seen wearing a bowler hat.

One of Greenock's earliest motor charabanc owners was Harry Carter of 8 Cathcart Street who was also a fruiterer. VS 1024 was a 19-seater 20 h.p. Albion of the early 1920s, photographed in Westland Drive, Glasgow, prior to its delivery from Albion Motors of Scotstoun. It is of typical charabanc design, with a door to each row of seats and a fold-down canvas hood which could be pulled up during inclement weather. At this period other charabanc operators in the town were Peter Beaton of Crawford Street; W. Davidson, Inverkip Road; David Service, Cross-shore Street and Edward Welsh, Port Glasgow Road.

Greenock & Port Glasgow Tramways supplemented their tram operations with bus services. SD 9186 was one of ten similar new Leyland solid-tyred SG11 types which were loaned to the tramway company during 1925 and 1926 by their larger associate, the Scottish Transport Co. of Kilmarnock, pending delivery of a fleet of Daimler single deckers which had been ordered. The location of this view has proved elusive.

The 'Pioneer' motorbus service was jointly owned by Walter Lucas (later provost of Port Glasgow) and Walter Pollock of the Port Glasgow Motor Co. GD 288 was one of several similar Albion 24-seaters bodied by Northern Counties of Wigan and is seen shortly after delivery in 1925. It was photographed at Princes Pier on the company's original service to Carnegie with the Clyde Shipping Co.'s buildings visible behind. The names of the crew are unknown.

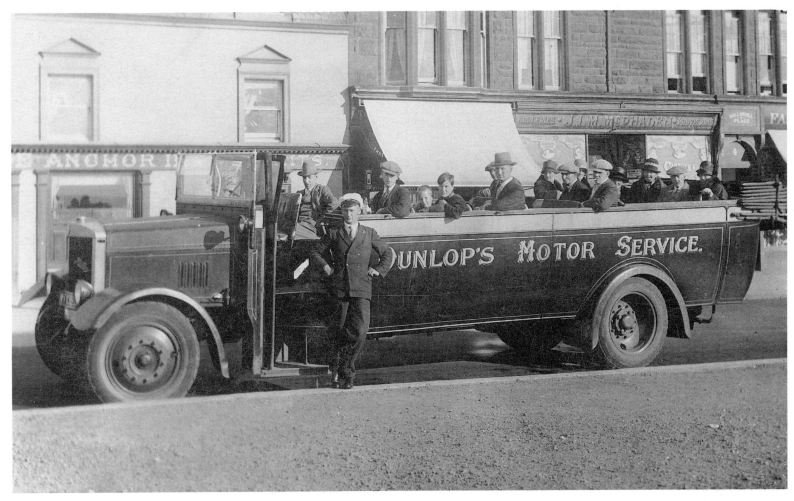

Dunlop's Motor Service was a well-known Greenock bus company which had operated the Kip Valley route between Greenock and Largs since the early 1920s. Prior to World War I, Dunlop had also been a removal contractor in Greenock, based in Duncan Street. In the earlier years of his business Willie Dunlop purchased Halley vehicles almost exclusively, until the Yoker-based commercial vehicle builder went out of business in the mid-1930s and he was no longer able to do so. Leylands then found favour. Seen here at the Largs pierhead stance in the late 1920s is VS 1065, a typical Halley charabanc of 1926, with the hood folded back to allow passengers to enjoy the summer sunshine.

Gourock-based bus operator Frederick Pyefinch originated in Kempock Street as a motor hirer and blacksmith. He started a bus service between Greenock and Largs in the mid-1920s in opposition to Dunlop of Greenock and Whatmough of Gourock, selling his business to the acquisitive SMT Co. in 1932. VS 1122 was the last vehicle purchased for his fleet. It was a 31-seater Guy and one of the largest single deckers in the area when it was bought in 1931 – at that time the usual seating capacity was only 26. Bodywork was built locally by John Mitchell & Sons of Grey Place, Greenock and incorporated a hood which could be folded right back on a sunny day – as seen here. The photo was taken at the Largs pierhead terminus, with owner/driver Fred Pyefinch and his conductress.

BURGH OF GREENOCK.

OMNIBUS DRIVER'S LICENCE. No. 78

Fred W Pyefinch

residing at *20 Manor Crescent, Gourock*
is hereby licensed as a Driver of an omnibus till 27th May, 19 30 , on condition that he complies with the provisions of the Bye-laws for the Regulation of Omnibuses made by the Magistrates on 26th March and confirmed by the Sheriff of Renfrew and Bute on 6th July all in the year Nineteen hundred and twenty-six.

Certified by me,

Andrew Nimmo

Town Clerk.

36

Prior to the regulations governing nationwide licensing of services, drivers and conductors brought about by the Road Traffic Act of 1930, various burghs throughout Scotland had their own independent licensing system in place for bus drivers. Greenock was one such town and reproduced here is the licence issued to Fred Pyefinch.

The Glasgow terminal in the late 1920s was in Carlton Place for bus services to Greenock and Gourock, either via Renfrew, Bishopton and Langbank or the inland route via Johnstone, Bridge of Weir and Kilmacolm. This scene shows the suspension bridge across to Clyde Street in the background with VS 272, an AEC owned by the Scottish General Transport Co. at the stance. Scottish Transport was based in Kilmarnock and had built up a network of services throughout Ayrshire and Renfrewshire. The Glasgow to Gourock route was operated from their depot in Clark Street, Paisley, where husband and wife team of driver and conductress, Mr and Mrs James Highet were based. Note the long racks of tickets, each of which was a different colour according to the fare value, and which were duly cancelled with the 'bell punch' on the cash bag strap. This emitted a gentle 'ding' when a hole was punched in the ticket.

In the late 1920s there was fierce competition on the route between Glasgow and Gourock via Renfrew, Bishopton, Langbank, Port Glasgow and Greenock, with three main bus owners each providing a 15 minute frequency on the service. Today there are no through buses on this route. The rival operators were the LMS Railway, with a depot in Largs, Gourock-based Harold Whatmough's blue 'Pullman Service' (see inside back cover) and R. & W. Fergusons' 'Victoria Pullman' from Renfrew and later Inchinnan, where the Fergusons built a new garage, which was later occupied by Western SMT when the 'Victoria' buses were acquired by that company in 1931. Whatmough also sold out to the SMT group and his Cardwell Road depot was likewise used for many years by Western. HS 4854 was one of several similar Albions in Fergusons' plum-coloured fleet. This one was new in 1927 and fitted with bodywork by Cowieson of Glasgow.

A late 1920s view of Port Glasgow showing Fore Street from the end of Church Street. Prominent is Port Glasgow town hall, with new flats under construction opposite. The old houses to the right were demolished long ago. Transport interest is provided by one of Whatmough's 'Pullman Service' Reo buses disappearing en route from Gourock to Glasgow, and Port Glasgow Tramways car no. 20 bound for Ashton. This was one of the 30 original electric tramcars which replaced the horse-trams in 1901. A horse-drawn cart is also visible, which was still a relatively common sight with local carriers in Scottish towns even into the 1950s.

The final tramway operation in Inverclyde took place on Monday 15 July 1929. This scene shows no. 10, the last car leaving Cathcart Square for Ashton, with Provost John Drummond at the controls and general manager R. B. Herbert at his side. A fleet of Leyland Titan double-deck buses, one of which is seen here, replaced the trams. Car 10 had been one of the original 30 open-top trams built for Greenock & Port Glasgow Tramways by Brush of Loughborough and which replaced the old horse cars at the opening of the new electric system in 1901. Today the buildings behind the bus and tram are home to the Clydesdale Bank and Yorkshire Building Society respectively.

This scene from the late 1930s shows some of the Western SMT bus crews outside the old Western depot in Cardwell Road, Gourock, which had previously been occupied by Harold Whatmough's blue 'Pullman Service' buses. CS 3367 is in the black and white livery used by Western at that time and was one of 40 Alexander-bodied Leyland Cheetahs delivered in 1936.

A long-established privately-owned coach hire business in Greenock was Alex J. Doig & Son whose premises were first in East Shaw Street and latterly in Roxburgh Street. Doig was also a coal merchant and general contractor in the town. Shown here is VS 5270, an Austin coach with bodywork by Mann Egerton of Norwich which was delivered in 1950.

JR 9333 was an older coach operated by Doig's. It was a Duple-bodied Bedford dating from 1939, and had originally served with an operator in Northumberland. The picture was taken in April 1949 outside Hastie's Engine Works in Princes Street, Greenock.

BAG 93 was a Bedford 'O' type lorry owned by Western SMT and used for collection and delivery of spares and general inter-depot work. It is seen in 1949 opposite Western's Cardwell Road depot in Gourock (see page 22). This had originally garaged Harold Whatmough's 'Pullman' fleet of buses, which operated from Gourock to Glasgow and Largs to Greenock. The premises are now occupied by Duncan Fisher van and truck rentals.

Dunlop's Motor Service of Greenock used this former US Army wartime Dodge as their service vehicle. It ran on Greenock 'limited' trade plates 008 VS and was photographed near Dunlop's depot in Holmscroft Street in 1949. As with the Dunlop buses of that period it featured the Red Indian's head as a motif.

The Greenock Motor Services fleet carried an attractive dark red livery relieved with grey bands. VS 3634 was a 1938 Leyland Titan TD5 with Leyland 'highbridge' bodywork, and is seen here at the Grieve Road terminus in Lyle Road during August 1948. Visible behind it is VS 4358, the first of six Burlingham-bodied AEC Regal single deckers delivered in 1946 and specifically used on local routes which involved passing below some of the many low railway bridges in the Greenock and Port Glasgow area. Today of course the Nissen huts are long gone and council housing is now all around.

VS 3066 was also a Leyland Titan, but a TD4 model delivered to GMS in 1936. Moreover it had Leyland-built 'lowbridge' bodywork with rows of four-abreast seats on the top deck and a sunken offside passageway which often caused lower deck passengers to bump their heads when leaving the right-hand side seats. It is seen in Drumfrochar Road, Greenock during April 1949 with driver Tucker and conductress Thomson.

Wm. Dunlop's service between Greenock and Largs was acquired along with his buses in 1945 by the Western SMT Company. Amongst the older vehicles in the fleet was TR 6216, a Leyland Titan TD1 which had been new in 1929 to Hants. and Dorset Motor Service of Bournemouth. In 1946 the original Leyland body was replaced by Croft of Gallowgate, Glasgow, which extended its lifespan for a few more years. This photo dates from April 1949 and was taken at Dunlop's Greenock terminus at the courthouse in Nelson Street, adjacent to George Square. The livery was cherry red and cream but was soon to disappear, since although Western kept the Dunlop fleet as a separate entity for a few years, from around 1950 all buses received the Western name and colours when due for a repaint.

As with the photograph overleaf, this view was also taken at Dunlop's Nelson Street terminus. CK 3959 departed on a sunny Sunday afternoon for Largs in June 1949 after posing with the crew for Hector Soutter's camera. This was a Leyland Tiger TS1 which had a rather unusual pedigree, having started life in 1928 with Ribble Motor Services of Preston. It was sold to Western SMT in 1937 and its original Leyland body replaced by Alexander in 1944. It was transferred to the Dunlop fleet in 1946 and carried the 'Dunlop's Service' name, despite the firm having been acquired by Western SMT the previous year. Dunlop's ran as a subsidiary until 1949 when finally wound up and operations transferred to the parent company.

VS 1962 was a Leyland-bodied Leyland Lion delivered to Greenock Motor Services in 1931. This view in Dalrymple Street, Greenock (part of the former main road through the town), was taken in July 1948, shortly before the bus was withdrawn from service. The Leyland Lions were regular performers on the service to Strone Crescent and latterly proved notorious for boiling on the steep climb from the town centre up to Strone. Following behind is one of the new Guy Arab single deckers (see overleaf) which replaced older members of the fleet such as this Leyland. The GMS initials were revived in the 1990s by Arriva Buses for their services based at Inchgreen depot.

VS 4433 was the first of ten Guy Arabs to be delivered to Greenock Motor Services with Guy's own bodywork, which incorporated a mixture of front and rear doorways. Guy Motors, whose factory was in Wolverhampton, used a Red Indian's head with full head-dress as an emblem, and this was incorporated into the radiator filler caps on Guy vehicles, as can be seen here. These buses entered the GMS fleet in 1947 and became immediately popular with crews and passengers alike. This photo, taken at the top of John Wood Street, outside Port Glasgow railway station, dates from July 1948 and shows the Star Hotel in the background. The Star has not changed but the row of tenements in Station Road beyond has been demolished.

Many people will remember the no-frills 'utility' buses which were delivered during wartime when most materials were in short supply. These buses were pretty basic, and as may be seen were fitted with unupholstered wooden slatted seats which literally made quite an impression on one after a journey of any more than a few minutes. VS 4351 was a typical example of a 'utility' Guy Arab, bodied by Weymann of Addlestone in Surrey and delivered to Greenock Motor Services towards the end of the war in 1945. It is seen with crew in 1950 and the driver has removed the bonnet side cover

to reveal its Gardner 5LW engine. The destination 'Smithston' is little used nowadays. It referred to the former mental hospital, now incorporated into Ravenscraig Hospital, although the bus continued to Burns Square at the Oxford Road / Auchmead Road junction where this photo was taken. New municipal housing in the Burns Square area may be seen under construction beyond the bus.

Gourock pierhead has been a hub of transport activity since the days of the horse buses. This typical scene from 1949 shows two Greenock Motor Services double deckers prominent in the foreground at the 'local' bus stop (as opposed to the 'through' stops for the Glasgow–Gourock–Largs services). The first is VS 4868, one of six Leyland PD1s delivered in 1948 with very poorly constructed bodies by Strachan of London which necessitated rebodying by Eastern Coachworks of Lowestoft only four years later. Behind it is wartime utility Guy Arab VS 4349. Both have their destinations set to return to Woodhall; certain journeys continued beyond the pierhead to Ashton and some to Lunderston Bay on fine weekends. Western SMT buses outside the post office

are BAG 156, a Brush-bodied AEC Regal on the 'low road' service to Glasgow via Renfrew, and BSD 409, a Northern Counties-bodied AEC Regent working the 'high road' via Kilmacolm to Glasgow. Carriages of British Railways trains are visible in the background at Gourock railway station.

The opening of Western SMT's new bus depot at Inchgreen took place in November 1955. These premises replaced the former Greenock Motor Services depots at Dellingburn and Ladyburn, the former Dunlop's Motor Service depot at Holmscroft Street and Cardwell Road depot in Gourock which had originally been the base of Harold Whatmough's 'Pullman Service' (see page 22). More recently Inchgreen depot changed ownership to Clydeside and then Arriva Buses. 1955 also saw the arrival of a new breed of double decker in the Western fleet – the Bristol Lodekka 60 seater. Pictured at the Inchgreen opening is 1151 (GCS 237), the first to enter service on the Greenock local services and still carrying its delivery trade plates. Third from the left in the official group is William Sword, general manager of Western SMT.

Climbing the Clune in 1955. GCS 213 had been newly delivered that year to Western SMT for their local operations in the Greenock area and was numbered 1128 in their fleet. It was a Guy Arab IV with body by Northern Counties of Wigan and is seen on a school special at the top of Port Glasgow's steep Clune Brae, passing the now-demolished old toll cottage. This would surely be a listed building had it survived.

A Sentinel steam waggon, but an earlier model than those supplied to Rapid Road Transports shown in the lower picture on page 40. This was an early 1920s example of a Standard Sentinel 3½ ton tipper, built by Alley & McLennan of Shrewsbury (until the First World War they were built in Polmadie, Glasgow) and registered there as AW 3108 prior to delivery to Port Glasgow Gas Dept. The slogan painted on the side reads 'Cook, light and heat with gas. Gas coke price ___ per ton delivered in bags'. The location is believed to be the railway sidings at Blackstone, Port Glasgow, with a load of coke being tipped into a Caley goods wagon.

This dignified fleet of Rolls Royce hearses was operated by Greenock Central Co-operative Society in the 1940s and 1950s. They were all second-hand, mostly dating from the 1920s, and had been purchased from a variety of different previous owners. Registration numbers from the left are XO 326, GG 1446, LK 4509, EC 4678 and G 5055. The location is outside the Greenock Co-op undertaking department in Terrace Road at the Regent Street corner.

Greenock Co-op, or to give it its full title Greenock Central Co-operative Society Ltd., operated a fleet of Albion lorries in its transport department. Co-operatives throughout Scotland tended to favour Albion commercial vehicles, since they were economic, hardy and reliable (the Albion motto was 'Sure as the Sunrise'). As may be seen on the cab doors of the lorries, the registered office was at 12 Roxburgh Street, but this photo was taken outside the Co-op bakery in Regent Street at the junction with Mearns Street. Also featured on the lorry fleet was Greenock's emblem of the green oak tree. This view taken in 1936 shows, from left to right, VS 2865, 2863, 3011, 3131, 3010 and 2867, all of which entered the fleet during 1935 and 1936.

Below: Albion lorries owned by Gourock Ropeworks leaving the factory in Robert Street, Port Glasgow and turning into Glasgow Road. Leading is HS 4811 of 1927, followed by HS 5301 of 1928. This photo was taken in 1936 to mark a special occasion as the lorries were carrying ropes for delivery to RMS *Queen Mary*, then being completed at John Brown's Clydebank yard. The Gourock Ropework Co. was established in 1736 (in Cove Road, Gourock) and had a close association with Clyde ships and shipbuilding through supplying ropes, sails, twine, covers and nets to the industry. 'Birkmyres Cloth' was also produced for hatch covers, tarpaulins and tents. Sadly, the business closed in the late 1970s.

Above: The other famous Cunard 'Queen' was also supplied with equipment by Gourock Ropeworks. This scene from 1940 shows Albion lorries delivering the hawsers from Port Glasgow to Clydebank in time for *Queen Elizabeth*'s maiden voyage that year. These included eighteen 9" Manila mooring ropes each 100 fathoms in length and four 2½" life lines each 120 fathoms long. This was wartime of course and restrictions dictated the masked headlamps and white-rimmed mudguards on the lorries. These were all Albions of various ages, led by AHS 749, a CX2 model of 1938 owned by the Gourock Ropework Co. Ltd. (Birkmyres Cloth) and followed by ABM 903 of 1936, belonging to haulage contractor D. McNaught & Co. of Glasgow. The final two were 1935 Albions which were also members of Gourock Ropeworks own fleet.

John Walker founded his sugar refining business in Greenock around 1850, with the original sugarhouse situated in Upper Nicholson Street. This scene from over a century later shows VS 8268, an Albion Clydesdale artic. with Homalloy cab new to Walker's in 1957 and finished in the once-familiar navy blue livery of the transport fleet. It is cautiously leaving the narrow exit from the loading bay in the now-demolished West Shaw Street refinery but will stop by the kerb while the driver haps down his load with the tarpaulin visible on top of the hundredweight bags of sugar. Greenock's last remaining refinery, owned by Tate & Lyle, with whom Walkers had been associated since 1928, closed in August 1997 thus ending a long connection with the sugar industry in the town which spanned over two centuries.

Jagger's lemonade was popular not only in the Greenock area but throughout Renfrewshire. As a boy in the 1950s I remember their turquoise delivery lorries calling at houses in my Paisley street. Robert Jagger started a factory in Prospecthill Street, Greenock, in 1911 where the company remained for most of its life before redevelopment caused a move to Baker Street for a period until the business closed around 1980.

The upper view shows VS 990, a Ford delivery lorry used in the mid-1920s by Jaggers when their horse-drawn wagons were being ousted by motorised transport. The back and sides of the lorry made advertising easy and the signs read 'Try our sparkling hop ale', 'Champagne ciderette' and 'Brewed stone ginger beer'. The rear shows the name and address 'Robert Jagger, Botanical Brewer, 7 Prospecthill Street, Greenock'. The later vehicle is VS 3258, a Commer of 1937. This lorry has 'Jagger's brewed drinks supplied in half-gallon jars' sign-written on the door. These jars were commonly used before glass bottles became popular and often people would keep them for use as hot water bottles to warm their beds.

Jas. Pollock & Sons of Chapelton, Port Glasgow, were originally haulage contractors in the horse transport days. Their first motor lorry was one of the ubiquitous Ford Ts, which doubled as a primitive passenger carrying vehicle with bench seats which could be fitted when the occasion demanded (usually at weekends). Shortly after the Second World War all motor vehicles were in short supply with much of their production destined for export only. In August 1946 Pollock was fortunate to take delivery of CHS 593, a brand new Austin 5-tonner finished in the company livery of dark blue. It is seen carrying an equally new Austin 8 four-door tourer on an advertising campaign for the Port Glasgow Motor Co. which was the main Austin agent in the town. The photo was taken in Queen Street, Port Glasgow at the rear of Lithgow's East Yard.

Many Inverclyde folk will remember the striking red and yellow liveried Rapid Road Transports lorries which were operated by the McEwing family. Business commenced in Jamaica Street, Greenock in 1923 with a couple of steam waggons hauling a wide variety of goods for such well-known local customers as Hastie's, Scott's, British Charcoal, Tate & Lyle, Gourock Ropeworks, Rankin & Blackmore and Lochore & Ferguson, to name but a few. The haulage business was wound up in 1983 but Gordon and Allan McEwing continued to service commercial vehicles at their premises in Chapel Street, Greenock until 1996 when they finally retired. Seen here outside the Sentinel factory in Shrewsbury prior to delivery on trade plates are two steam waggons (the Sentinel company always used the double 'g') supplied to Rapid Road Transports in the early 1930s.

Market Place with Parish Church, Kilmacolm

Kilmacolm lies within the Inverclyde area and this view from around 1906 represents wheels in the village. It was taken from the market place looking up the High Street past the parish church; Barr's Brae leads off to the right. The only visible traffic is provided by two horse-drawn farm carts, but nonetheless the proportion of motor cars in Kilmacolm at that period was probably higher in this affluent community than any other in the county. Note the warning signpost which the Scottish Automobile Club has erected just outside the church wall. It reads 'KILMACOLM: Please drive slowly'. This was significant at a time when cars were still outnumbered by horse-drawn vehicles and local authorities rarely considered themselves responsible for any form of traffic sign.

Three schoolboys sit and watch the trains go by in Kilmacolm station in May 1956. The one pictured here was the daily 2.55 p.m. freight train on its way from Greenock's Albert Harbour to Greenlaw goods station in Paisley. The class 3F 0-6-0 locomotive was a former Caledonian Railway engine which continued in service with British Railways until the early 1960s. Beside the boys is one of the weighing machines once familiar on many station platforms. On some types a penny was dropped in a slot and out popped a card on which your weight was printed. Often these were collectable picture cards sought after by schoolboys, and now more often by adults.

Another view of the leafy station at Kilmacolm. The 2.04 p.m. passenger train from Glasgow (St Enoch) calls on its daily departure for Greenock. This was in August 1954 and the locomotive on this occasion was 4-4-0 class 3P no. 54440, which was also a former Caley engine. Of interest is the semaphore signal at the front of the locomotive, the arms of which could be altered according to the train's destination (in this instance Greenock Princes Pier). Also of note is the fact that the engine appears to have lost its front number plate. Thanks to the coming of the railway in 1869, Kilmacolm developed considerably as a commuter village, and although the railway ceased to operate in 1983 its presence over the years had contributed to the expansion of the community, and Kilmacolm is now one of the most desirable residential districts in south-west Scotland.

The exterior of Wemyss Bay station is equally impressive as its interior, seen opposite. This view probably dates from shortly after the new building opened in 1903 and shows some of the horse-drawn carriages which brought passengers to and from the trains before the days of the motorbus. Note the smart appearance of the uniformed coachmen with their top hats. Thankfully, Wemyss Bay station is classed as a grade 'A' listed building and remains virtually the same today as it appeared almost a century ago.

Wemyss Bay station was the terminus of the Caledonian Railway Co., with their steam trains bringing custom (as the electric trains still do today) to and from the connecting steamers which sailed to Rothesay. The railway arrived at Wemyss Bay in 1865 and when the line was doubled in 1903 the original station was replaced by this magnificent mock Tudor structure designed by architect James Miller. This Edwardian view shows the impressive glass roof to advantage and the hanging floral baskets which were formerly a feature of this fine station. It is 12.35 according to the station clock and a Caley loco has just pulled in to platform 3 with a train from Glasgow, whose passengers set out towards the covered boardwalk down to the adjacent pierhead. Wemyss Bay station underwent an expensive restoration in the early 1990s to its former glory, which should allow us to enjoy its unique character for many years to come.

Wheels of a different kind, but nonetheless just as important as those on road vehicles were familiar in Inverclyde for over a century. They were the paddle wheels which plied the pleasure steamers operated by a variety of companies which called at the piers at Gourock and Greenock. Paddles churn the waters of the Firth in this view of the Caledonian Steam Packet Company steamer *Galatea* as she reverses from the pier at Gourock in 1903, with Kilcreggan seen on the Dunbartonshire shore beyond. *Galatea* was the flagship of the new Caley fleet when she arrived shortly after the railway reached Gourock in 1889, no less than 48 years after trains first reached Greenock!

Approaching Greenock's Princes Pier in 1903 from Dunoon is the Glasgow & South Western Railway paddle steamer *Mercury* of 1892. Visible beyond is another paddler, the *Lady Clare*, heading for the Gareloch.

Princes Pier Greenock opened for pleasure steamer traffic in 1870 and was home base for the vessels of the G&SW Railway fleet. Seen here about 1905 is PS *Mars*, which was built for the company in 1902 and served as a minesweeper during World War I, only to be accidentally run down off Harwich in 1918 by one of our own destroyers. Horse-drawn carriages await custom outside the fine pier buildings, which were opened in 1894 but sadly demolished to make way for the construction of the container terminal in the late 1960s.

A similar scene at Princes Pier from the opposite direction, looking west to the distant hills of Argyll. The time on the clock tower is 10.45 and a well-laden PS *Caledonia* is about to cast off and set sail on the Holy Loch service to Kilmun, Strone and Blairmore. The year was 1929 and the then ageing vessel belonged to the Caledonian Steam Packet Co. (under LMS Railway control since 1923). The ladies seated on the bollards in the foreground wear the cloche hats then in vogue, while cloth bunnets were the favoured male headgear.

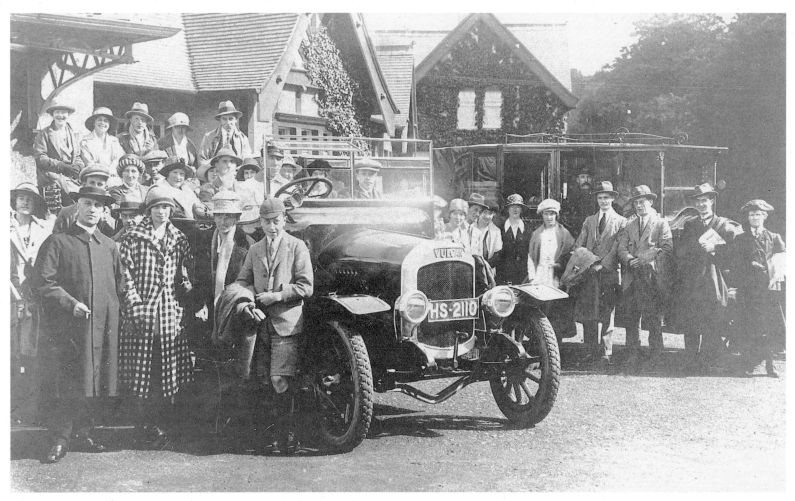

Wemyss Bay railway station around the mid-1920s. Local garage proprietor and automobile agent John Pearson had started hiring horse-drawn coaches from the station forecourt about 1912, and later progressed to motor vehicles. HS 2110 was a Vulcan charabanc painted in a striking red livery which he purchased in 1921 for hiring and providing excursions from Wemyss Bay. The picture shows a group of ladies and gentlemen on what was probably a church outing. The Edwardian Renault landaulette taxi alongside was also owned by Pearson, whose family currently still operates the village garage. Motor vehicles were registered with 'HS' identity letters in Renfrewshire and 'VS' in Greenock Burgh.